Skiing: From Greens To Reds, and beyond.

Skiing: From Greens To Reds, and beyond.

The book that accompanies the Bobski Youtube channel of free lessons

BOB TRUEMAN

VALENTINE TRUEMAN PUBLISHING
WELSHPOOL U.K.

Contents

Acknowledgements

My thanks

BOB TRUEMAN

My thanks for so much skilled help, to

John Shedden for advice, photos and diagrams. Even more for giving up his time to edit much of it, thereby helping to rid it of clumsy expression, confusing advice, and Trueman-esque misperceptions! Any remaining are mine, not his.

Martin and Julia Webb at spinningyourdreams.co.uk for cover design.

Ellis Brigham (ellis-brigham.com) for permission to use cover photo.

The book was created in Pressbooks (pressbooks.com) with much appreciated support from them.

What really matters ?

Regain your confidence: dispel apprehension: get back your self-esteem

BOB TRUEMAN

I started skiing at age 46 and like everyone else went to "ski school". I soon learned that it was not an effective teaching medium. The idea that watching an expert facilitates emulating what they do is ridiculous. I could watch Roger Federer play tennis until I was blue in the face and all I would learn is to hold the tennis bat at the thin end.

Traipsing down slopes at the end of a long snake of skiers was equally ineffective. So I tried a few private lessons but since they were given by ski instructors employing the same idea they didn't work either.

Because skiing is so addictive that it ought to be a listed Class A drug, I then did what everyone else does and took to "getting the miles in" hoping that would work, but all it does is embed poor skiing habits.

So in 1993 at the age of 54 I had been skiing for eight years. Hopelessly. Then I met an Alpine Skiing *Coach*. A very different animal. In one week he blew away the fog of confusion about how skiing works. In one more week he changed not only my skiing but my life.

With a lot of work and persistence (in the face of insults and sneering from skiing teachers in the instructor training milieu) I became an internationally qualified skiing *coach*.

*But can **you** really improve?*

For 25 years or so I've been teaching skiers who want to improve and thought they couldn't. Skiers still apprehensive or fearful; skiers who had lost confidence - who want to ski knowing they're in control - who are confused about *how* to improve - who have lost self-esteem, or think they're too old.

THOSE are the things that matter. They matter much more than the skiing. Finding the *process* that helps you ditch your fears, rebuild your confidence, and come to realise that YOU can do what you thought maybe you couldn't, has been my number one aim. One pupil kindly wrote "I hope you realise the good you do" - and she meant more than just the skiing she meant what she could take into the rest of her life and how she felt about her self. No one has said a nicer thing to me.

And this is what has given *me* the greatest satisfaction I've ever found in the mountains, and I've spent a lot of time in mountains! A chap called Zig Ziglar once said - "You will get all you want in life if you help enough other people get what *they* want".

Perhaps why I've succeeded at this is because I was just the same. Skiing didn't come easy to me. I *proved* that you don't have to be young, unimaginative, bold to the point of lunacy, or indeed even male - what you need is the *right process* and the willingness to persist. My job is to help inspire you, give you the right support and encouragement so you can bring about the changes you want.

It gives me the best of feelings when I see my pupils change their self-belief and realise they *will* achieve their goal no matter how old they are, or what gender.

The essence of the difference in this approach to learning.

You will encounter all sorts of seemingly childlike ideas and images in this book; and in the videos on the Bobski channel that accompany it. Why are they here?

The reason is that they are my imagery-based translations of the serious study of ski and sports teaching that was done some fifty years ago by a small group of PhD physiologists, physicists, and psychologists from universities and elsewhere.

These studies showed that because humans are psycho-physical creatures in whom there has to be constant to-ing and fro-ing between our minds and our physical experiences, we need simple "tools" to get the maximum benefit out of the process. You are going to encounter 'friendly little beetles', 'cuddly little moles', and other creatures.

They are all here for very good reasons. I could quite easily have used tough-sounding words and phraseology typically found in ski instructors and instructor trainers – I know them all. I could have talked about "getting a *harder* edge"; "learning to love the *fall* line"; "get 'em on their edges and remember speed is your friend" (!) all that kind of thing.

But I have not. They don't work. They are there primarily to establish the instructor's seeming superiority. The proof is that after almost a hundred years of alpine ski school teaching there are so few really competent recreational skiers, despite the fact that skiing has got much easier because of ski design improvements and new materials technologies.

All I ask is that you bear with me. Trust me: at least enough to give this new (for you) approach a fair chance to bring you what you want – skillful skiing at an advanced level. I think it was Henry Ford who said "You can if you think you can".

I really hope you enjoy what you find here.

Regain your confidence: dispel apprehension: get back your self-esteem

BOB TRUEMAN

Skiing: From Greens to Reds, and beyond.

A skiing workbook for every recreational skier.
Originally developed for members of the British Int'l Ski Coaching Club (BISCC):
For Man or Woman: no matter your age.

Introduction.

This book is written specifically to accompany the series of **free** ski teaching videos on the **Bobski Youtube Channel.**

Lost confidence. Confusion. Lost self-esteem. And Fear.

Beyond ski school lessons few skiers carry with them a clear idea of what to actually *do,* in order to get their skis to behave as they want them to. The purpose of this book is to explain that skiing is achieved by making specific *movements* with your body, arms, and legs. It explains what the key movements are, how to make them, and when to make them.

This short book introduces you to extremely simple

and highly effective "games" and processes that will take you from Greens-to-Reds – and much further. It is written for recreational skiers who want to ski better.

For over twenty years I have slowly developed a ski teaching / ski learning process for the BISCC* that has worked for the members far better than any of their previous encounters with either ski schools or their own attempts at "getting the miles in". [* *Additional note – membership of the BISCC is open to anyone over the age of 18: the average age of members is a l-o-n-g way over that!]*

If you go sub-aqua diving you have to go to on-shore classes first to get a background knowledge of how the process works. Thankfully they do not take you into the water straight away. But if you go to ski school your instruction only commences when you arrive on the slope, and it is limited to the time you are in the resort. This guarantees maximum anxiety potential – you are already *in* the environment you may find challenging before you start – which constrains learning.

This is a limitation that can be overcome. You can make a huge amount of improvement in your skiing with "work" done both *before* and after your skiing vacation. My job as club coach has been to develop coaching services accessible *throughout the year*. This has been made possible by advances in computing such as emailing, blogging, and occasionally Skype.

In addition I have been able to develop imagery concepts and practice "games" (they are included in this book and in my first book – **"Ski In Control"** – available from Amazon Books) that help you do very effective practice **at home**, any time you like – with advice available all year. You don't need a ski slope in order to improve your skiing, *you can make significant changes while at home.*

Plus, like every other sport, so much of skiing is inhibited by the psychology of the situations in which we do it. In competitive sport much of that is aggravated by thoughts of 'losing' or performing badly: in recreational skiing it is often a fear of having an accident. So I have made a great deal of information available to members through a series of "White Papers", on how to control one's *self* through mental game planning and the like.

I wrote this second skiing book, and made the videos it supports to give better ski coaching a broader distribution for *all* skiers, not just our members. But the books and the videos do more than that, much more. While taking you toward expert skiing they help you overcome –

Lost confidence. Confusion. Lost self-esteem. And Fear.

A word search of scores of letters from member pupils saying how successful our courses had been for them showed how important these issues are. They repeatedly mentioned –

- *how they* ***gained confidence, or re-gained lost self confidence.***

- *the benefit they got from being helped to* ***understand how skis work.***

- *how feelings about themselves improved not only on slope but back in ordinary life as well. Their self esteem was lifted.* ***They no longer felt they were "no good"***.

- *they mentioned how* ***simple*** *and comprehensible the process had been, when hitherto (sometimes for years) it had been a mystery to them.*

- *and they specifically mentioned conquering their* ***fear*** *of the slopes, which had rather spoiled their fun for years.*

Their experiences of ski schools and so-called 'academies' had not satisfied these needs.

These are psychological processes not physical ones; on the one hand, issues of mental comfort (confidence, self-esteem, fear), and on the other, the learning process – (better understanding and simplicity.) In my opinion these are issues of far greater importance than the skiing itself. They concern the real *you*, in ways that ski schools cannot.

Before they found my approach to ski teaching our members had encountered a self-reinforcing loop in which they had been **confused**by skiing and found it unfathomable; had lacked an **understanding**of *why* and *how* it works; this in turn undermined their **self-confidence.** That translated into **apprehension** because the process seemed unpredictable and dangerous, and this had led them to feel inadequate and to **lose self-esteem.** These are very important issues, more important than the skiing: they concern the real *you.*

They could see better skiers on the slopes but couldn't see or understand what those skiers were doing that was different to what *they* were doing. So how could they change? It is impossible to divine how to ski better by watching, unless you have been *trained* to watch – like a coach. Folk concluded that they were somehow never to be expert skiers. They felt in some way sub-standard. That was not true even though they felt it.

Those are the ski teaching issues that I have always felt needed to be addressed in order to find a more effective **process** than skiers had previously encountered. It is the process that matters, far more than the immediate outcomes. If you have the right process all you then need is persistence.

I find skiers come with one of two mindsets. There are skiers who care about *what* they ski or where – how many kilometres in a day; did they get down every last piste; what was the steepest slope; how many bars did they visit? They care more about what they ski, and less about *how* they ski. That is perfectly legitimate, it is their holiday. And of course they don't need me – or any other teacher; they're not trying to get better.

There are other skiers who really care ***how*** they ski. For them, skiing is an important form of self expression. They want to find a pathway to being the best they can be. Being mediocre and skiing a lot of miles gives them no satisfaction. What satisfies is being on the pathway to expert level skiing. Improving every season.

Feedback from skiers like this showed that the ski school experience didn't suffice. Like me for my first eight or nine years of skiing, they did not know that there is a teaching resource *beyond* ski schools and the so-called 'academies'.

Two questions stood out from the analysis of members' letters.

1. **What is involved in understanding skiing and how skis work?**
2. **What is involved in enhancing the *learning process*?**

Question 1:

What makes a ski work and makes skiing possible is quite simple. To give you an understanding of it only needs a few simple explanations of the underlying physics. These are best conveyed in analogies of everyday-life experiences. It is not rocket science. I will do this, and you will find it clear and understandable.

Question 2:

How to improve your learning of skiing? Improving your learning process isn't complex either, it just requires –

- My helping you to take *ownership* of the learning process, through what you *feel* and *notice*, not what you *think you see*.

- My making the necessary skiing *movements* easily understood and easy to remember, even when you are under some stress. (Skiing is effected by making small movements whilst you are in motion).

- Providing you with information and practices *prior* to getting on slope.

- Ensuring you learn on slopes that *you* consider safe.

- Making progress in small steady additive increments

This is the rationale of the teaching process this book lays out for you.

I.

How [and why] skiing works.

BOB TRUEMAN

The film, the Youtube videos on the Bobski channel, and this book are aimed at two different readers.

1. Firstly recreational skiers who want to become truly expert and are not happy to remain mediocre skiers.

2. Secondly those *instructors* and ski schools who would like to improve the *teaching* they offer, to provide a better service.

The film and *this* book are not intended to *fully* explain how skiing works, although I do explain *why* I have included some of the games we will play. What *this* book does is run you through a series of things to **do** that are *proven* to work; never mind why. They are very simple (not necessarily easy) and most folk learn them quite quickly: pupils typically make huge transformations in just one or two weeks' courses.

If you want a deeper understanding of skiing and to manage your *self (your psychology)* in order to do it better, search on Amazon Books for "Ski In Control: Bob Trueman". It's all in there. That book concerns itself more with how to manage and control your mind and gives a fuller explanation of why skis behave the way they do.

Briefly – why resistance is not futile. (A short explanation of how skiing works)

Forty or so years ago I was driving through Sweden in the late afternoon one March. The ice melted during the day but by about 3 pm it re-froze. Some of the bends were dry, some had frozen run-off water on them. On the dry bends I had perfect control, on the iced bends I was all over the place. Why? What was the difference?

The *simplistic* answer is that the iced bends were slippy, but that answer begs the question; it doesn't address what the *force* was that directed the car safely round the *dry* bends, but not the iced bends. The *simple* answer is *resistance.*

On the dry bends the road surface offered resistance to my car's innate desire to keep going in a straight line. When I turned the wheel friction between tyre and road surface provided resistance which deflected the car's motion. On the iced bends there was no friction, and therefore there was no resistance, so my car kept trying to kill me by not going round the bend.

Skiing also works because of **resistance**. Specifically *snow resistance*, not friction.

Snow has almost no friction, but unlike car tyres skis thankfully don't work by using friction. What they do is to cut into the snow surface and provide a *tilted* *platform* for the ski, *against* which we – as riders of the ski – can brace. (Hint: "edges" don't come into it, at all; of which more later).

Skiing is not about slipping around on snow – that's a complete misunderstanding – skiing is a snow **pushing** game. Find a way to push against the snow and Mother Earth will use the snow to push back, and the ski gets pushed around in an arc. The ski carries us round that arc. That way *you* get to control where you go; like me on the dry bends. You don't "turn the ski" – it carries you. You don't do "turns".

Everything we do on skis – **everything** – is concerned with what happens at the interface between the sole of the ski and the snow surface. The more positive that contact is between them, the more control you have. Lose that close contact or lessen it, (for example at the ski's tip by leaning back), and you will lose some element of control over your direction.

Ski school and beyond.

Very few skiers continue with ski school after two or three years. Most of us then hope that "getting the miles in" will help us improve but instead that locks in bad skiing habits that do the opposite – that limit our development and lock us into mediocrity. Better teaching is the key that opens that lock.

But *coaching* is not easy to obtain – hence the videos and this book. I skied for eight or nine years before I discovered there was such a thing (back then) as the English Ski Council, and a comprehensive coaching process available to recreational skiers. It was a transformational discovery for me.

In my first book "*Ski In Control: How to ski* ANY *piste anywhere in full control, man or woman, young or old*" I explain how skis and skiing actually work and how to control your *self* to help them do it.

Some of my pupils have been instructors but in many instances they have been middle-aged and older men and women with many years of skiing behind them, who thought they'd never be any good. And in many instances they not only learned to ski very skilfully but changed their view of themselves and their potential: discovered that no one needs to be a lost cause. Found they were capable of much more than they thought.

My new videos show you a series of very simple steps that enable you to control precisely what your skis do. You are not asked to watch and *imitate* in the way most ski schools demand: instead they show you what to do, and much more importantly what to *feel* and when to feel it. In high quality skiing what really matters is **what you feel** – what you are *aware of*.

The importance of "feedback".

In the late 60's early 70's expert sports coaches recognised that skiing is a form of "system". The study of systems and how they change tells us that any purposeful change in a system has to be driven by feedback that is *recognised by the participant, is prompt, accurate, and meaningful.* You need this to know *how* to change and it is lacking in almost all ski instruction which instead supposes you can learn by watching. Did you learn to drive by watching? No you learned by finding out what small movements you needed to make as your car went along. Without recognisable, accurate and meaningful feedback ...... disaster!

If the feedbacks – the information flows – are *delayed not prompt, false not accurate, inaccessible, or meaningless*, then the way the system will change will be nothing more than random; as likely worse as better. You see the effects all around you every day in government departments; stock exchanges; in every system.

John Shedden and Dennis Edwards designed the "Intention/ Attention Feedback Loop" (TM). It is the fastest and most direct route to skilfull skiing (and much else). It forms one of the key features of how I teach. It's also how Olympic level coaching is done nowadays.

You are likely to have done countless ski runs and <u>not been truly aware in real time of what was happening.</u> Never felt a thing. If you didn't *feel* what was going on, in real time – you weren't *aware* – the chances of getting better were very small. You'd need a lot of luck; things could just as easily get worse as get better.

The psychologist Carl Jung said "Until you make the **un**conscious conscious, it will run your life – and you will call it fate".

We need something, some kind of tool to help us *easily* connect with the feedbacks that will help us improve. We need an easily learned method of *noticing*: of becoming *aware*. And *what* we notice needs to be simple and instant and accurate. Technicalities won't do. Not because we are stupid, but because in the real-life situation of skiing, there is so much going on. Sometimes the stress levels are so high that without *simple* feedback signals we will not be able to cope. And we won't improve.

Now it's good to understand but it's not enough on it's own. You need clues **as you ski** that you can easily access, to tell you exactly what is going on. Only then will you progress to become an expert skier. Have no doubt – you *can* become an expert skier. The ones who are, are not different from you.

Learning how to learn.

I have a difficulty with our education system. It teaches *stuff.* It doesn't teach us *how* to learn: it just assumes we all come into existence somehow knowing. Well, we don't: we have a forty million year old brain that comes without an instruction book. I think that it is a shame that we are not taught *how* to learn – if we learn how to learn, we could learn *anything.*

For example, how many people know the three stages of learning something – Cognition (thinking it through and understanding), Association (the practice phase, during which at the beginning we manage something one time per hundred, and at the end one hundred out of a hundred), which leads to phase three – Autonomy (when what we have now learned we do without thinking about it at all).

When you know these stages you can rid yourself of that old feeling that "I ought to be better at this / why aren't I as good as that girl over there". You can put your progress into context. This is psychologically very empowering. If you can't do something right now, you can take an intelligent approach to it and acknowledge that for example – "This is new to me, I'm currently in the thinking-it-through stage" – instead of running yourself down by saying "I'm no good".

If you try to learn something physical such as skiing by *watching* someone else who is expert you'll just get frustrated. Ski instructors tell you to watch them: they should be watching you. When I started I didn't find watching a jolly good skier show me how good she was at all encouraging; like most of the rest of the class I just moaned that "Oh Lord, I'll never be able to do that!" In fact the *better* they were, the worse it was.

This doesn't only apply to skiing, you could watch Tiger Woods playing golf until you ran out of breath but you wouldn't improve your golf. There's too much going on that you can't see. When Woods drives a golf ball 450 yards what you *see* is the *outcome* of what he did: the sum total of a mass of small invisible body movements. The movements were what he *did*, the drive was just the *result* of what he did. He would charge you a lot of money to disclose what he did!

Humans poorly absorb large amounts of data. We learn best and quickest by constructing "stories" and by "connecting the dots" using analogies and metaphors. Very few of us learn best from highly technical explanations, loads of numbers, or a series of pictures.

This applies to everything we learn, so ski teaching ought to take this into account. It should not rely on simply following someone else down the slope or telling folk to "get them on their edges". (Small tip – you don't, indeed cannot, ski on "edges" we'll come to that shortly).

Skiing is dynamic.

Things get more complex as slopes steepen, and snow gets more varied. Life is made more difficult still by anxiety and the need to be more agile and responsive to all the changing forces that go with constant movement. And this is exactly when the most ancient part of your brain – your amygdala – is screaming at you not to move at all!

We spend almost all our year standing upright, vertically above our feet, with our weight supported on our heels, on a dry high friction, level horizontal surface. What comes over us? – we then conclude that it would be a great idea to strap ourselves onto a pair of "extended feet" about six feet long specially designed to be very slippy, and point ourselves down a friction-less slope.

Small wonder then that many feel a bit scared. Being scared inhibits learning. And yet skiing can manifestly be done, and done in safety and it's fun. This is a further clue that friction has nothing to do with it - there must be a hidden secret. There is!

Dynamic but small and subtle

Skiing is dynamic, in fact it works best when it is more dynamic and less static. But here is a thing - you may have seen TV footage of car rally driving or some other seemingly wild event. The outside shots of the cars look terrifying - cars leaping off the ground, snow and gravel spraying in all directions. Cars never going in the direction they're pointing. Loads of noise and mayhem. Ski racing looks similar.

But now look at the in-car shots of the drivers. Complete calm. Fixed unblinking stares. Almost no bodily movement. Very small turns of the steering wheel and tiny gear shifting movements. And therein lies a clue to skilfull skiing

Like Tiger Woods or the rally drivers, what you need to do is to make VERY small precise movements of your arms / legs / feet etc. You establish some forward flow and then within that flow make those movements. Movements in motion. Like the rally cars, these movements recruit powerful forces from mother earth that steer your progress and give you access to the control you want.

I'll shortly be telling you exactly what small movements to make and how to make them. You will be surprised by their power.

Childlike.

My coaching method takes account of this need for small movements. It takes account of ways in which we can learn how to become *aware* of both the movements and their outcomes. In other words it gives you access to the needed feed-backs. It puts *you* in the driving seat, and it does it in ways which would otherwise often seem childlike.

I make the movements very easy to memorise and associate with: they are commented upon by pupils from years back, as still being what they use to guide their skiing especially if they encounter difficulties.

Regrettably my experience has been that most ski *instructors* find them too childlike for their egos to accept: most of them are quite young after all. But I make them childlike and very simple on purpose. When we are faced with skiing down a slope there is more than enough going on already, without using opaque technical terms or trying to copy someone else.

What we need is a toolkit of simple physical *metaphors* that are not scary, are very easy to comprehend and are highly memorable. Easily brought to mind.

Then we must take into account that learning *anything* is best done in small linked steps made in the least challenging circumstances we can find. We do best doing one small thing at a time, adding them together to build a solid structure. That is the process that this book will take you through in such a way that you can even coach yourself.

SIMPLE IS BEST. My favourite phrase.

2. Getting a posture that works.

Your posture – the most *fundamental* fundamental

I don't like "basics". When things begin to go wrong people refer to "going *back* to basics". This suggests that they think basics are something you have to get through (perhaps miserably) and then you can leave them behind with a sigh of relief and get on with the proper stuff.

I prefer fundamentals. You *never* leave fundamentals behind. Slalom World Champion Tom Stiansen uses the same fundamentals as me. He never left them behind. He uses exactly the same ones as me, but does them better.

Let's consider your posture. *I call it your "Ready For Action" posture (RAP)*

You can't adopt a single posture and maintain it, stiffly, at all times of course. Skiing is dynamic so it involves a lot of "creative wobbling" in a similar way to, say jumping from stone to stone to cross a stream. You can't actually do that "in balance", but you are constantly moving from one "balance" to another "balance".

There are some absolutely fundamental aspects to skiing posture that you need to do well. You could think of them as forming your "safe house" – the place you are always trying to return to. That "returning to" is a continuous *process* and it is that process which matters like my stream analogy. It matters more than the RAP itself. It's the difference between trying to be **in** balance, and a kind of "fuzzy" balanc**ing**.

Stand a brick on its end and will be **in** balance, but it's incapable of balanc**ing**.

The Ready For Action posture isn't like the one you adopt for about 50 weeks of the year when you are living on a level high-friction surface at home or at work. Because of this it will not at first feel "natural". But when you are skiing, "natural" is exactly how you need it to feel. Automatic.

We can't *see* ourselves when we are skiing. So we could do with a way to accustom ourselves to what it *feels* like when we are in the "safe house" ready for action posture.

You own a completely free, marvelously functional and readily available every-day-of-the-year piece of equipment to help you with this. It is your full length bedroom mirror. Take a few minutes on a few days a week each week throughout the year in front of your mirror and it will get you accustomed to this posture. It will help you feel comfortable with it and to do it well. It will be worth an extra week's skiing, for free.

It is very important to do it well if you really want to improve. The RAP is the cocoon in which your skill slowly develops and will finally emerge as something truly elegant – even beautiful. Like a butterfly. (I'm still working on mine by the way. I'll get there one day!)

RAP your FISH.

We humans use mnemonics to help us remember things. Here's a really useful one. We wouldn't want to carry a fish home unless it was wrapped in something – so let's spell WRAP wrongly, let's spell it RAP (your Ready For Action posture).

Now to your FISH.

F stands for FEET – have them roughly hip-width apart, neither jammed together nor very wide. Just comfortable as you would normally wish to be.

I stands for INDEPENDENT LEG ACTIONS – your legs may need to do the same things but at different moments, or different things at the same moment. Just be ready for that.

S stands for a "sloppy S shape" that your body and legs will roughly form when looked at from the side. I say "sloppy" because as mentioned above we don't want to be stiff and rigid. You will need to flex your ankles, flex your knees, and flex at your hips so that your back **inclines forward** (not upright, like we stand 50 weeks of the year). Slouch.

H is for your **hands**. All they need to be is LOW and WIDE. They don't need to be stuck out in front of you, and they should not be held high. And you don't need your arms to be in an exaggerated aggressive "gorilla" shape either. Gently relaxed arms and subtle, is better.

If you stand and allow your back to tilt or incline forward a little, and "slouch" your shoulders, and then completely relax your arms they will dangle loosely *just* ahead of your torso. Only an inch or two. That's all you need. From there all you do is spread them a little wider and have your thumbs and first finger joints pointed toward the floor.

You've got it right if when you are looking straight ahead you can just see your hands in your peripheral vision. Imagine Big Ben's clock face just ahead of you with its centre level with your navel. And now imagine your hands level with the "five" and the "seven".

Be aware that while just now these may seem like "nit picking" points, they really are not. Every one of them adds to establishing a skiing posture that will make a huge difference to your performance; especially as you progress to increasingly challenging slopes. Practise it a lot – below, I tell you how!

That issue of having your back inclined forward is one of the key things that make practising this posture so important. When you are on a downward sloping snow slope it will at least for a while seem a crazy thing to do – to be feeling you are leaning down the slope. Your unconscious mind will be screaming at you to lean back. That is the **worst** thing you can do.

Imagine if you will, walking in summer in the country down a slope when the grass is dry and polished. If you lean back, what happens? Your heels will shoot away ahead of you down the slope and you'll land on your bum. So we must practise. If you cannot get used to the feelings of the best posture in the warmth and safety of your bedroom, you will certainly not find it on a mountain. Now is the time!

Here's how to use your bedroom mirror. *(Go to the Bobski YouTube channel and check out the ones entitled "Getting in Shape" and "Gone F-I-S-H-ing)*

First you could face the mirror directly. Check your "RAP FISH" notes and ensure your feet, hands etc are correct. You won't able to check your "sloppy S" yet. When you are sure you have your posture right, *close your eyes and* ***feel*** what that correct posture feels like. Get accustomed to it.

Open your eyes, vary it slightly, and go through that little game again because you are going to need to be dynamic when you get to the slopes. The more times you do this the sooner and the better you will accustom your mind and body to the feelings. What you are doing is burning-in essential neural pathways in your brain that you will all the more easily access when you are on the slopes. You need to FEEL, you can't *see* yourself while you're skiing.

[Have you ever watched ski racing on TV? Sometimes they will show the skiers in the holding area waiting for their turn to go. Very often you will see the skier, crouched, eyes closed, and swaying from side to side. She is doing exactly what I'm suggesting here but in her imagination – she's *feeling* every arc, every rise and fall of the piste; and she's doing it by running those neural pathways one more time to anticipate what it will be like. We can do the same, but in the safety and comfort of our bedroom.]

Now, turn sideways on to the mirror. Check your "sloppy S". Make sure you flex your ankles, your knees and at your hip (not your waist). Then ensure your back is inclined forward at an angle that is **at least** that of your shins. Now turn your head to face the same way as your body, close your eyes and check the **feelings** you've got.

From now on you can play with all those angles. Look in the mirror, flex your ankles knees and hips either more or less, turn to face forwards (the way your skis would now be going) and repeat. And repeat.

Soon you will be able to stand sideways on, **not** look in the mirror, adopt a chosen set of angles and only then take a peek – and you'll have it right. And it will feel natural. You're on your way!

One further point. If your pelvis is at a comfortable *neutral* angle – neither tilted up or down – your back will be rounded. You need it to be rounded. You don't want it hollow. If you took a ski pole and placed it down your spine, you'd want it to touch in only one place not two. You don't want a hollow back.

If your hips don't feel comfortable when you are in t his posture stop doing it for a bit – who wants to be uncomfortable? Older skiers will recall ski teachers telling them to tuck their bottom hard under them. I was told to think of holding a coin between my cheeks. Ridiculous, you can't even walk like that never mind ski!

If your ski pole would touch in *two* places then that hollow back is a dead give-away that your pelvis is tilted too sharply downward. When it is, it will inhibit your legs rotating in the hip sockets, and this will stop you skiing well. Just allow your pelvis to be in a neutral position, like it usually is. Then if you tuck your tummy in a little, your back will be rounded: there's no reason to strain.

Yet again, I urge you to **practise** until you become aware of these feelings. When you get back on the snow slopes you will be well rewarded for your efforts in the warmth and safety of your own home.

Good luck. And stick at it.

A word about boots.

I cannot stress too strongly that in order to ski expertly you **must** be able very readily to flex at your ankles, and sometimes quite considerably. Most skiers cannot do this – their shins are always too nearly vertical – and the reason is that they have got the wrong idea about ski boots. They buy boots that are too "advanced" and too stiff. They believe this stiffness gives them stability – doing them up really tight makes them feel secure: but the truth is that over-tightness will do the opposite because it constricts how you can move.

Ski boots are already stiff and they get stiffer as they get colder. In the shop they are softer than they will be all day. Add to this that most skiers do them up much too tightly at the top, and they then make matters worse by cranking up the so-called "power strap" so tightly that their ankles will hardly flex at all.

If you do this, you will never achieve a skillfully workable Ready For Action posture. You do not need your boots overly tight and stiff in order to be stable and safe. In fact the opposite. For sure, *racers'* boots need to be because of the very high forces involved, but they are excruciatingly painful and only work properly at very high speeds.

I recommend that sometimes when you are working with your bedroom mirror, you do so in your ski boots. That way you can experiment with having your boots both very tight and very slack, and check the difference. You will be amazed. With them too tight you can't get your shins to go forward by flexing your ankle and knee. This means you can't get your *back* to incline forward except by adopting some weird posture akin to sitting on the potty, with your shins vertical and your bottom stuck out behind loading the *tails* of your skis, when it's the tips you need to control.

Two more things that can cramp your style. Your ski poles.

There is a rule of thumb that ski shops use to select the length of ski pole they give you. Unfortunately it tends to make them give you poles that are too long.

Poles longer than optimal tend to make you stand

too upright: they make adopting the best Ready For Action posture difficult, and when you're concentrating on something else they sneakily encourage you to stand upright with your back perpendicular, and then to sit you back. You will then be more likely to move your centre of gravity onto your heels, and therefore onto the tails of your skis. You don't want that – it's your ski *tips* you want to control.

On a course I was giving in Austria once I went with pupils who needed to rent equipment. When the shop owner handed them their poles I interceded and asked for shorter ones for them. To my surprise he became quite angry and defensive, saying *he* had been doing this for 30 years. He even got sarcastic and brought out some children's poles. Why he reacted like this I don't know.

Here's a suggestion, something that will make you wiser than them. Let the shop give you the length they think fit. Then use them for a day. Take them back at the end of the day, and ask for a pair 10 cms shorter. They will likely express surprise and try to impose their will on you, but do it anyway; you're paying. Use that pair the next day.

If at the end of that day you don't feel comfortable with those, take them back and ask for a pair 5 cms longer than them (the half-way point). I'll put money on either of those two shorter options, helping you maintain a better Ready For Action posture. And you will have learned something useful that you will carry with you for the rest of your skiing days.

3. Squeeze a beetle - get control

The smallest movement with the biggest result.

Be in a good Ready for Action posture and with this one smallest of movements you could ski down almost anything. Safely. The game we're about to play recruits such powerful forces from Mother Earth you could almost have a good skiing career with nothing more. This is all about making the small "movements in motion" that I mentioned earlier when I was talking about rally drivers and ski racers.

Here's the game. (Childlike) *You can play much of this in your bedroom too.*

Pretend that I got into your sock drawer and I put a little friendly beetle about the size of a Ladybird into each sock. They each crept down towards the end and each of them snuggled into their sock just where that little hollow will be, underneath where your big toe joins your foot. There is just enough room for them under your toe in that hollow.

What we're going to do is to gently compress them; first one, to go in one direction, then the other to go in the other direction. Not to harm them, we don't want them dead: we just want to squeeze them a bit.

While you're in your room – or anywhere else that's safe and warm – I want you to adopt your Ready For Action posture. Facing the mirror will be best to begin with. Being in your stockinged feet would also be best for now.

Choose one "beetle", it doesn't matter whether it's left or right.

The game is to find a way to *slightly* compress the chosen beetle more than the other. Let's say we first choose the *right* foot's beetle. (This is subtle stuff – not that easy to explain, so bear with me.)

At slow speeds, or while static in your bedroom, you can only increase the pressure on your beetle by adding a small amount of weight to it. The workings of gravity insist on it. So *some* weight has to be transferred over it, by you. What is *very* important is *how* this is done.

FIRST and foremost you need to ensure you are flexed at the ankle, knees and hips, and **your back is inclined forward**. Remember, it's your *right* beetle we're addressing here. Same would apply when addressing your left one.

Now, with your hands low and wide, and only by a minute amount, *very* slightly twist your torso (to your right) to place your *head* over your beetle, whilst continuing to look ahead as if you were skiing. It's a small subtle movement, not a gross one. Ensure you can then feel you are squeezing down on that beetle more than the other.

NOTICE THIS – as you do this, be aware of your *left* hip. Well executed you will feel your left hip move ever-so-slightly forward, of your right hip, and equally importantly *inward (leftward)* toward the centre of what would become a leftward arc.

Let me put that again in a slightly different way because it really *is* that important. The postural issue here involves forward flexing at the hips – inclining your back *forwards.* Stand upright and this isn't going to work.

Then the KEY TAKEAWAY is *to avoid transferring the centre of your **pelvis** (your centre of mass), over towards the beetle.* Your head goes over it, but your centre of mass goes the other way.

Why have I gone to so much effort to explain this is such detail?

It is because if misinterpreted this movement smacks too much of the absolutely incorrect instruction – too often seen on the slopes, and demonstrated – of simply transferring your weight sideways over one ski by leaning sideways, or bending sideways at your waist. That is wrong.

What is wrong with it? The big difference is that this better way loads the inside of your ski tip (via your beetle) and tilts the ski, so giving you a stable tilted platform: the other (bending or leaning sideways) not only doesn't load the tip, it more significantly eliminates any tilt. This increases the risk of **slipping** because the ski tip will not incise the snow, or worse will dig-in the outside edge and tip you over.

If you were skiing and not standing on the bedroom floor, then by playing this game with your *right* beetle, it is to the *left* that your skis would take you. The better you can get your pelvis to move toward the centre of that forthcoming arc the better skier you will be because you will exercise far more control. It should be clear that when squeezing your *left* beetle, the same applies but in the other direction.

The less you move the better. Investigate if you can *feel* that little tiny bit of extra pressure exactly where that little hollow is with the beetle in it, and that tiny bit of movement of your hip.

Practise this with both beetles (one at a time) until you get good at it. Become your beetles' best friend. Take them to the slopes with you.

Beetles on the ski slope.

In your bedroom motion was absent. On the snow slopes we have it – we can allow our skis to begin to slide. But this introduces a further element – timing. *When* do we want to squeeze our beetle and move our pelvis slightly toward the centre of the arc? It's important.

I recognise that what we are about to do will seem like a "beginner" description, and you are probably already a skier. So forgive me, I am not trying to tell you how to ski, I am trying to help you *change*how you ski, by helping you change your *perceptions*of skiing. Perhaps the most limiting factor in skiers' development is that most skiers don't have in their mind a precise idea of what they intend to *do*.

We need to do this "beetle squeezing" when it is perhaps hardest to do it. Skiing is counter-intuitive, what works is what the ancient instinctive part of our brain thinks *won't* work. We need to do this beetle-squeezing precisely when the ski passes the point on the arc when it is transitioning through pointing straight down the hill. This is when the ancient fight-or-flight part of our brain is screaming at us not to. Tell it to shut up. Our amygdala may have saved us from Sabre-tooth Tigers, and dangerous cliffs 40,000 years ago, but it knows nothing about skiing.

Picture this: you have chosen a very gentle slope, the very gentlest you can find; one with no threat in it whatsoever. You will be in the best Ready For Action posture you can muster. Picture yourself skiing very slowly *across* the slope. You will be doing something to stop your skis from heading downhill – probably just tilting them slightly. Just now it doesn't matter how you are achieving it, you just are.

Now I want you to stop doing whatever you are imagining that is. You will find your skis begin to drift downhill of their own accord. Let them do it, they will now be describing an arc in the snow. The hard part of doing this is the feeling that you are choosing to encourage your skis to head off downhill. But you are not. They are not going *downhill* they are drawing an *arc* in the snow not a straight line.

At the exact moment when they are passing through that-straight-down-the-slope moment, gently squeeze *one* of your beetles whilst flexing your ankle, keeping your back inclined *forward* and putting your head over that outside ski somewhere on the ski between the front binding and the tip. Not directly over your 'beetle' but ahead of her. Only your head, and keep looking forward. Beaware of the pressure on your beetle (it will slightly increase). Just as you did in your bedroom practice, feel if you can notice your hip move toward the arc's centre, and then WAIT. – spelled W.A.I.T! You need do nothing more. On the slopes, where you have motion, you will find that tiny feeling of your pelvis moving towards the inside of the arc, and forward, is SO much easier than it was in the bedroom!

Your skis are already describing an arc before your sink onto your beetle, and by sinking so slightly onto your beetle you make the skis <u>continue</u> to describe that arc. They will NOT head off downhill taking you to your doom. All you have to do is WAIT, and the ski will continue round until it takes you across the slope in the opposite direction to the way you were first going. Then you can do it all again, using the other beetle.

There are very good reasons – scientific reasons – why this happens, but this book is not concerned with them. If you would like to know why, so you understand it more fully, search Amazon Books for "Ski In Control by Bob Trueman".

But if you are satisfied just to have it happen – to have it *work* – this is all you need for now. Remember though, you will need to practise it until it becomes automatic. Also remember that everything gets more complex as the slopes on which you ski get steeper. So for quite a while be happy to stay on green or at the very most, blue slopes. Even if you can already get down blacks. You're trying to change something in your skiing; don't complicate matters. I promise you, your learning curve will be steeper when the slopes are shallower.

Don't complicate things.

With this in mind – not complicating matters – I want to mention one more thing. When I introduce this simple "beetle" concept to pupils and they begin to practise it, far too many of them introduce something else – something uncalled for.

They sink slightly on their "beetle" which ensures the arc will continue as they want: so far so good. **Then** for some reason they pick up the inside ski and plonk it down to make sure it goes parallel with the outside ski which is already doing the work. A small reminder just in case – the outside ski on a left handed arc is your *right* ski, and on a right-hander it is your *left* ski. These are the skis that give you your support.

This "lift and plonk" usually happens with skiers of some years experience, and it is usually because years before some instructor left them with the idea that "parallel" skiing is somehow 'better' or more 'advanced' than non-parallel skiing. The skier is anxious to avoid skiing with their skis in a wedge format in case anyone sees them.

In fact, skillful or non-skillful skiing happen irrespective of whether the skis are parallel to one another. *Making* the ski go parallel is not a sign of skill, in fact it is the opposite. There is absolutely no need at all to do this lifting or sliding the inside ski parallel to the outside ski.

Parallel skiing is not a sign of better skiing. If you *make* your skis go parallel it is usually a sign of insecurity – a strong desire to get the arc to happen quickly and suddenly: to get it over with. This leads to the oft-seen "oh shit" 'turns' – sudden jerky changes of direction done at the last minute just before the edge of the piste looms.

There is nothing wrong with feeling insecure – we all do sometimes – but now you have decided to become a skilled skier, becoming *aware* if you do this, will be valuable to you. No judgements, just feedback.

Smooth rounded arcs that are allowed to take their time are **far** more stable, safe and enjoyable. They give you a much better and more stable platform. They are a sign of skill whether your skis are parallel or wedged.

Skiing with your skis parallel to one another is an outcome, not of skill, but of *speed.* Nothing more. As you ski faster your skis will go parallel, Mother Earth will see to that. Just leave them alone and concentrate all of your attention on the outside ski. It will serve you well.

Here it is in a diagram. This shows you when to squeeze your beetle for this first stage of the game. It also shows you the next two phases, covered in the next two chapters.

When you get to those, refer back to this diagram and by Chapter 5 you'll have the full picture of what you can do with your "beetles" and "grapes", and importantly *when* to do them. Specifically, where it says "extend your leg to *press* (or, if you like, to "*push")* your beetle" – this will be the *other* leg (the other 'beetle' under your toe) from the one you have been squeezing your "grape" with. If you were sinking onto your right hand grape by flexing your right leg, for a leftward arc, you would now extend your *left* leg to press your left-hand 'beetle' into the snow. This will give you immediate control of your left ski, and initiate the new (now, right handed) arc.

Diagram showing when / where to use your "beetles" and your "grapes"

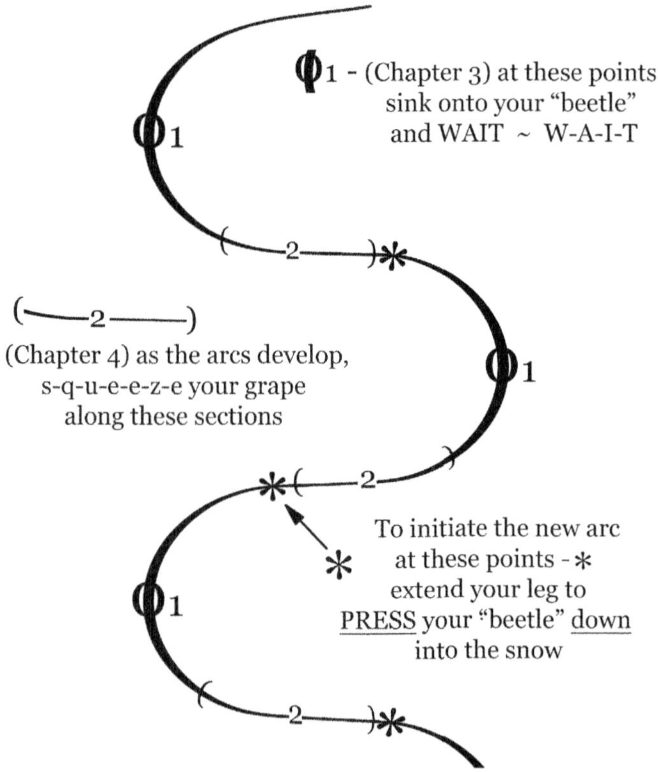

Skiing movements and when to make them

(Diagram kindly created for me by John Shedden – any errors are mine alone).

4. Feed your beetle - get even more control

Here's the second game – Beetles need feeding!

These games we play work in sequence – first one first, then the second and so on. One small step at a time. And once again I make no apology for keeping it childlike and simple. This is what really works when you're on your ski slope.

One further plea – if you are already a skier who can get down most things, please don't under-estimate this approach. It may seem childlike but you will find that it is the quickest and most assured way of changing your skiing for the better. If you are one of those skiers, all we're trying to do is to make something already good, rather better.

A young recently retired Royal Marine pupil on one of my courses, admitted to me that for the first two days he only pretended to take part because it didn't seem "manly" enough; but he said it was only after joining in with the spirit of the thing that he really changed his skiing. And he certainly did. (He astounded the guide we had with us!)

While making the movie of my teaching one of my pupils, Phil, admitted he was sceptical to begin with: he had the grace and courage to say on film that he was glad he dispensed with that. Just "getting down" things no matter how clumsily gives you little satisfaction – being skillful gives you a lot.

I've been in your sock drawer again. The day after I put beetles in your ski socks I realised they'll need food. I got into your sock drawer again and this time I rolled a grape into each one of them. But grapes don't have legs so they didn't get as far down as your beetles.

In each sock the grape only rolled as far down as your instep. When you put your socks on you'll find in the *right* sock your grape is located exactly under the *left* hand side of the arch of your foot. In the other sock it's the opposite. These are small grapes, they don't spread right across your foot. They sit under the arch, half way along it.

Now you have a beetle under each big toe where it joins your foot, and a grape under the *inside* side of the arch of your foot. Shortly we'll give that a bit of a squeeze as well.

Here's what you need to do.

As before, pick the very gentlest slope you can find. If it's not too crowded pick the beginners' slope: don't be proud. The shallower the slope the steeper will be your learning curve. And the slower you ski, the faster you'll improve your skiing: because it gives you time to become *aware* of these new feelings.

Awareness is everything. Remember Carl Jung? – "Until you make the **un**conscious conscious it will run your life and you will call it fate". Always do what you always did and you'll always get what you always got.

Going back to our friendly beetle, let your skis drift into going downhill, same as before and at the moment they are pointing directly down, sink onto your one selected beetle by flexing your ankle. If it's your right beetle your right ski will carry you to your left, and if it's your left beetle your left ski will carry you round to your right.

I told you it would be simple!

The ski begins to come round in an arc because of what happens when you make the movement *you* make, and as you W-A-I-T it keeps coming round until it's pointing directly *across* the slope. The *force* which powers the arc is *the resistance from the snow* and it is this which is initiated by the movement you make. Note that in these instances we are using our weight to apply a small force to do the squeezing or pressing, by flexing our legs and "sinking down".

We can apply force by doing the opposite. When we extend (straighten) our legs we also apply force but this time by using our muscles rather than our weight. We'll come to it later, beginning in the next chapter.

Your job is to obtain and control the **snow resistance**. The ski will still be sliding forward, and now is the time to sink down just a tiny fraction **more**, this time to feel your foot gently squashing your "grape". You do this progressively *after squeezing* your "beetle".

When you have practised this numerous times you will begin to perceive that your ski reacts slightly differently. Done well, you will find a greater feeling of support and security from it. It comes round the arc even more positively. The arc may even tighten-up somewhat. Your ski will give you an even better 'platform' which you can now begin to "brace" *against*, (not stand *on* it).

Right now it doesn't matter why it works – it just does. (You can find out why by searching on bobski.comor more fully in my book "Ski In Control"). For now, just do it, and enjoy it. It's like magic. What is even better is that **it will work every time.**

And that's it for lesson 2. As I said before – but now with even more effect and certainty – at these very low speeds, if you get adept at the Ready For Action posture and these two very small movements (let the ski find the "flow" line, and then "sink") – never mind all the things that follow later – you will be able to ski almost anything. Well! Not fast, but who cares as yet – you will become skilfull.

The better you get at doing them, the greater the challenges you will feel happy to take on. It really is worth the effort – just take a look at my "pupils comments" section on www.bobski.com

5. How to Take charge!

How your "beetle" can put you in control just that little bit sooner than before.

You have been very careful not to hurt your beetle: you've treated her gently. This is fortunate because she will now be willing to help you even more.

There are two ways you can use your legs and feet to gently squeeze your beetle. You can do it the way we have so far, by a gentle extra sinking down (flexing your ankle and with as little other movement as possible remember). The **instant** you did this **you** took control.

There is another way you can squeeze your beetle. When you do your arcs by squeezing your beetle and then sinking on your grape, you end-up in a very slightly more folded Ready For Action position. With your skiing joints (ankle, knee and hip) more flexed. But you can't do that for ever or you would screw yourself into the ground. That slightly increased leg *flex* means that if you want it, you now have a small amount of leg *extension* available. You could *straighten* your leg a bit.

If you straightened your leg slightly, and slightly more quickly than you sank, (try it in front of your bedroom mirror) you would feel your big toe press on top of your beetle's back and press her feet more firmly into the carpet, or the snow if you're on the piste. Not for long, only for so long as your leg is straightening, but long enough.

What you will be doing is to push her a little more firmly into the snow. You could think of it as helping her get a better grip in it with her six little feet! That is certainly the effect – by doing this you get *immediate* control of the ski's tip. Again, at this stage it doesn't matter why – just trust me, if you do it, it will work. You get that control because your imaginary beetle is closely connected with your ski's inside ski tip.

By pushing your 'beetle' into the snow you will press your ski tip into it, and it is that which enables the inside of the ski tip to incise the snow's surface and begin to create the *platform* you so much desire. Why does this work? It's because you have obtained some *resistance* from the snow, to you motion.

Two questions arise – 1) which of your legs do you staighten? and 2) *When?* You can work this out and practise it – guess where? In your nice warm bedroom.

Taking control – earlier.

Imagine yourself back on the slope crossing it from right to left of the piste, and being supported primarily at least by your *right* ski in this example. When we first started you allowed your skis to *drift* into the flow-line down-slope; you waited until your chosen ski was pointing straight down; then you sank onto your **right** beetle to squeeze her a bit – she took you round in an arc to your left, and you WAITED; then you flexed the ankle and knee of the same leg a little further and squeezed her grape.

You were then coming to the end of that leftward arc so you've sunk on your right ski and your right grape. You decide you've had enough of that arc and want to go round the other way. The time to do it is either at the **end** of the current arc, as decided by you, or at the **beginning** of the next one (you choose) . Perceptive readers will recognise that if you are linking one arc immediately into the next they are one and the same of course.

Simple! You're now traveling from right to left across the piste and being supported by your right foot's grape

(you're executing a leftward arc). Just at the moment when you choose to change direction, focus your attention onto your **left** beetle again (because you want to be carried round to your *right* this time). Only this time push her feet more firmly into the snow by *straightening* your **left** leg – don't just let it drift this time. You will push your foot *down*. It can't last long because your foot won't actually sink into the snow, but it's enough for your beetle to get an instant grip.

Instead of waiting for your ski to *drift* toward downhill, you've now *told* it to go there when you tell it to. Then as before, as soon as it is in line with straight down, you repeat everything you've done before – sink onto your beetle (*same* beetle) and then your grape. **Remember** – you sink on the *same* leg you straightened. It's more like skipping than walking.

I know – this will be confusing for you at first (it certainly was for me all those years ago!) but you will work it out. Just keep going over the sequence I've written above, one element at a time to begin with, then link them together as you get more used to the ideas.

If you're already a skier you'll get to a point where it suddenly "clicks" and you'll likely say – "Why didn't he say that before"? The difference is that now you will be *aware*of what you are doing. You'll have a plan in advance, a *known*series of movements, and you'll be *conscious* of the outcomes. That is important and a very significant difference, and over time will enhance your skiing like never before.

Talk to yourself as you do it.

Nearly every skier I've taught find it helps. Let's start the new sequence of movements *after*you have flexed down and squeezed the grape.

Actually doing this on slope often confuses initially – take a look at Videos 12 & 13 (I think!) of my Youtube videos and you'll see what I mean – each additional step in the movements sequence adds to the difficulty of my pupils remembering it all. But persevere and it will come.

At the risk of repetition let's start the new sequence of movements *after*you have flexed down and squeezed the grape. You're coming to the end of that arc. The *next*movement will be to straighten the *other*leg (not the one you're squeezing the grape of).

Imagine yourself at that point and practise saying any of these to yourself and it will help –

"Press – wait – sink – squeeze" or

"Press – wait – beetle – grape" or

"**Push** *Beetle – wait – sink on beetle – squeeze beetle's grape – push new beetle".*

Or of course come up with your own, but saying it out loud as you ski is a great help to begin with, even if you get some odd looks! (Which you won't even notice!)

One final explanation ..

"Press (new beetle into snow) – wait – sink (on that beetle) – squeeze the grape – then Press (new beetle into snow)"

I know this all sounds a little crazy, but decades of teaching has proved that it really works. If you want to change your skiing for the better, knowing what movements to make and when to make them makes all the difference. Don't be shy give it a try.

Diagram showing when / where to use your "beetles" and your "grapes"

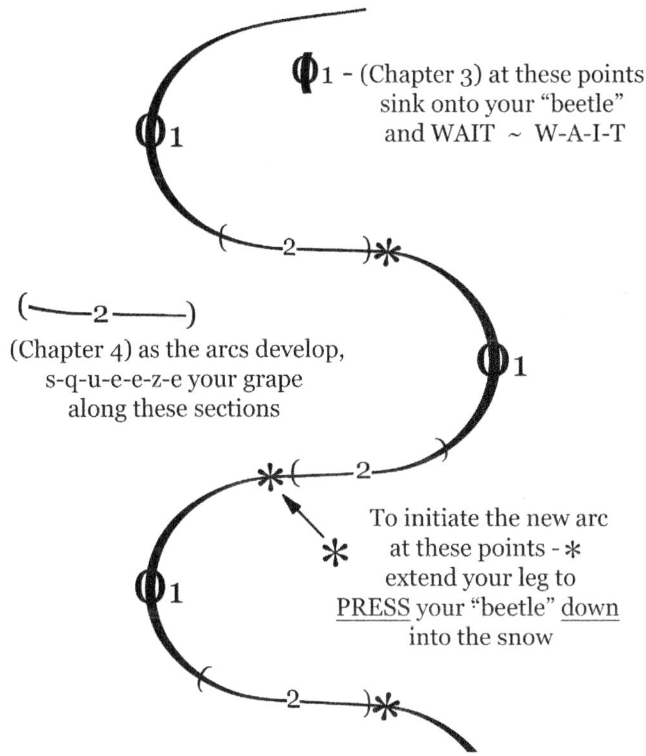

Skiing movements and when to make them

What you are developing is an ability to ski *rhythmically*. To be continuously flowing, smoothly. It's what every skier I ever met, really wants to achieve.

"A continuously linked series of well-rounded arcs".

This all runs counter to the old-fashioned instruction where you were told "There is *this* kind of 'turn', and *that* kind of 'turn', and possibly even more kinds of 'turns'. There are not. You don't *do* 'turns', and you don't need straight lines between them unless you have a specific reason. That's the trouble with "turns", in order to have them you have to have something else in between them. Inevitably that something is straight lines.

In a straight line you have less control. It's also not as much fun as riding an arc. Better by far in every way is to think of your skiing as a *continuously linked* series of well-rounded arcs. You can still choose their radius. You can still select their speed.

And now you'll be a 'proper' skier.

Your skis won't head you straight down the hill.

The instant that *you* decide you want to end this arc and start a new one, all you have to do is that small leg extension (leg 'straighten' if you like) with the sole intention of helping press your beetle so her feet dig in a bit more.

THIS IS NOT ABOUT "STANDING **UP**". It's about pressing **down**. Why do I say this? Because in your excellent new ready-for-action posture your back will be inclined forward – parallel to your shin or even more so. When you press your beetle *down* do everything you possibly can to avoid allowing your torso to come upright. **Keep it inclined forward.**

For no other reason than that you pushed your beetle's feet down into the snow, albeit very gently – from that very instant your new ski will *immediately* begin a new arc. It will start very gently at first but it will start without any delay.

Just like before in our first two 'games', as soon as the new ski points straight down the flow-line, then **sink** onto your beetle again by flexing your ankle and allowing your shin to press into the front of your boot – that feeling of the pressure on the front of your boot is your feedback mechanism that tells you that you have flexed your ankle. This will *keep* her feet in the snow. As the arc comes across the slope once again **sink** that little bit more onto your grape to help the arc finish off nicely.

Remember this very important point – because your ski is describing an *arc* from the *moment* you give it the instruction by pushing your beetle with a leg straightening, then at some moment later, for a nano-second it will be pointing downhill. That doesn't mean it's going to go there. It isn't.

Think of it in driving terms again – imagine you are driving your car round a nice dry bend: for a nano-second it may point straight at a telephone pole on the other side as the nose swings round. That doesn't mean it's suddenly going to go in a straight line and crash into it: why would it? It's the same with your ski – that apparent "point" in the arc isn't really a point at all; it has no more relevance directionally than any other point along the arc, of which there is an infinite number. Think of it just as a timing device.

Let's re-cap.

The story so far. We've identified two parts of our foot that matter. We have imagined a beetle in a hollow under our big toes, and a grape under the arch of our foot – not a big grape, it doesn't stretch across our foot, it's just under one side (the in-side of the arch). Same with our beetle you only have a big toe on the inside side of your foot. It's because of these facts that when you make these movements their effect is not only get resistance, but to do so by *tilting* the ski.

Here is the sequence. Do everything you can to do this every time you set off.

Every time before setting off get into your very best Ready For Action posture. Then **imagine** what you are going to do. Then,

Step 1: We started by *letting* our skis drift of their own accord into the flow line.

Step 2: When our chosen ski was swinging through the point on the arc that was straight down we *sank* onto our beetle ensuring our back remained inclined forward. And we WAITED.

Step 3: After we had waited for the ski to begin to come across the slope we *sank* onto our grape.

Step 4: We moved on, to take control earlier by *pushing* our beetle's feet into the snow at the moment we wanted to change direction. We did this with a leg extension.

Step 5: We then repeated steps 2 and 3 to control the completion of the arc.

When you have reached steps 4 and 5 the sequence will be "Beetle *(push)* – Beetle (*sink*) – Grape (*sink more*) and repeat". Lots of my pupils vocalise this as they do it. It helps.

OK, so you have imagined your way through the sequence now – **every** time before setting off get into your very best Ready For Action posture and then – do it.

So far, so good. So far, so simple! Far from easy, but really satisfying!

6. The importance of making your own routine

Why is all this worth doing?

I have introduced just two small imaginary devices so far – the "beetle" and the "grape". I have stressed the need to use them in the context of your best Ready For Action posture. Now you have something to work with, I ought to tell you the best *process* to employ as you work with them. *Process matters more than content.*

This brings us to Shedden's and Edwards' "Intention/Attention Feedback Loop" (The Int/Att Loop) ™. The human brain sends messages to our muscles, and receives messages from a variety of sensory systems that we have – smell, taste, hearing, sight, touch, plus the fancily-titled proprioception.

But it cannot do the two things at once. It can either be *sending* instructions along the nerves to muscles, or *receiving* feedback information from our sensory organs. It can do them rapidly in alternation, but not at the same time. Your brain uses the received information to modify the next set of instructions it sends back to your muscles.

From your practical point of view – working to become an *expert* skier – this has implications. It dictates an optimal on-slope *procedure* – a routine

– that works best for you. One that you will build-in to your skiing and never diverge from it. A superb example of creating and adhering to a procedural routine such as this, is any world class tennis player preparing to serve. Every one of them has their own rigid routine which they employ while they mentally prepare.

I can't resist quoting from my favourite sailing author Tom Cunliffe to drive this point home: it's about passage planning.

> Ill fortune will appear to dog the skipper of a yacht on a poorly planned passage. Fair tides will elude him; he will be unlucky with his wind shifts; the fuel on board will prove infuriatingly inadequate; and he'll miss the tide on the marina by just 20 minutes.

Here is how this aspect of mental preparation works, and how to use it in your own training. When you are practising to improve your technique and control, only ever ski short sections of slope – 200-300 metres at a time. Never ski entire runs. It has proved impossible for people to concentrate on these practices for very long at a time. It takes quite a bit of effort. And you need frequent reviews of what you've done. You also have to take care that you don't inadvertently practise "bad" habits.

By all means ski an entire run for fun of course, but when you do, don't expect to improve – indeed don't even **try** to improve. That's the "practice makes perfect" idea, or the "get the miles in" idea. Practice does not make perfect it makes *permanent.* Humans get good at what they do – practise the wrong thing and you'll get good at it. Then if you always do what you've always done, you'll always get what you always got. Beware! The point I'm making is that if you ski entire runs, something (quite likely not noticed by you) will begin going wrong and the result will be that you inadvertently practise bad habits, and get good at doing them!

What to do every time before you set off.

First **think**! **Plan.**

When you are training to improve never set off without a plan. I like to put it this way: your plan is to swap some of the skiing you've got for some skiing you'd like more. To swap the one for the other. S.W.A. P. – always **S**ki **W**ith **A** **P**urpose.

Decide **precisely** what you intend to do on the next short section. Only **one** simple action. Now you own a beetle and a grape you can choose whichever you like. Hitherto I would bet that you never had a clear idea in advance of a specific *precision* action you intended to *do.* For example, your Intention could now be "to start my new arc by pushing my beetle's face into the snow instead of letting the ski *drift* downhill". Believe it or not, that simple idea would be a very good, well defined intention.

Now if your brain is to obtain some useful knowledge fed back from your sensory systems, how will it *know* whether or not you succeeded in your intent? It is crucial that before you set off you know *how* you will perceive what is happening. You need to find a way to become **aware** of what is happening AS it does so. This is your focus of *Attention.*

In this case, your goal of pushing your beetle's nose into the snow, makes that easy. You won't be able to see it, taste it, smell it, or hear it. But you will be able to *feel it.*

Make it your habit to first of all – and *before* moving – to ensure you are in your best Ready For Action posture. I repeat, *before establishing any motion.* You may not maintain it but at least you will have started off in it. Gradually it will become your norm. Never set off without doing it: it's the aggregation of all these small disciplines that will set you apart from the great mass of skiers.

So, you set your intention, and you identify what will tell you if and when you achieve it. You could choose either to feel what you feel under your big toe, or perhaps the straightening of your leg, and imagine *when* you will feel it. The more detailed your imagining is, of what it will be like, the more effective you will be. It only need take a few moments – you won't miss much skiing! When you *imagine* you begin the process of "burning-in" those neural pathways. Then you adopt your RAP and without further hesitation, set off!

Let's pretend that you chose a different Intention. Let's say you chose *to sink* onto your beetle. How might you seek to *feel* that? Again, look for simple ways – either you could simply decide if you will feel the pressure under you toe where your "beetle" has taken up residence; or you could choose something that would have to happen if you were actually doing it. That something will be that your ankle must flex more, and your shin then needs-must press forwards into your boot. So you could let yourself be aware of "shin-pressure" instead.

How to do it.

You now have a clear precise intention. You have given yourself the opportunity to *imagine* what you'll be doing and what it will feel like, so now you can set off for the next, shall we say 300 metres. While you are skiing **do not think.** Do your best to just DO what you intended to do. And as you do, become aware of the feeling under your toe on each arc, or the feeling of your shin, or your leg straightening – whichever is appropriate. **Only onething please**. Never two.

At the end of that section, stop by the edge of the piste, and only then think back over what you experienced. Ask yourself – "what was my **intention** (be precise!); remind yourself how you were going to know – what had you decided would be your focus of **attention**; and then ask your self *did* you know? *Did* you feel it? How much or how often did you feel it? What happened as a result?

This is the time to be clear, simple, and honest with yourself. If you are honest you cannot give yourself an unhelpful answer. Your answer could easily be – "Did I feel it? *No.*" That answer is a great answer and is useful to you because it will help you on your next attempt. Even the question/answer "Did I feel it? I don't know" is useful – it shows that you *know* you don't know – it will help you find ways to change that. A man once said to me – there are too many people with answers and not enough people with questions.

The answer that is not useful, is to *pretend*. Or to "fudge". Or to answer a question you didn't ask. Don't pretend. And remember it's not *how* you felt, it's *what* you felt that is useful. It's not what you were *trying* to do that is of use to you. It's what you *did*. And no matter what the answer is, don't "beat yourself up" about it. Avoid making value judgements. Jean-Claude Killy one of the all-time greats said "Skiing is always to strive to be better, to extend your boundaries, but it's supposed to be fun – it's not an obligation".

Whenever I am working with pupils and I ask them *what* they felt, all too frequently they will tell me "If felt o.k." or "I liked it" or some such. Resist that – keep it simple. Do not "work it out" by thinking about it. Consider some of the games we've already played. We straightened our leg to push our beetle downwards. What you may have felt could be "pressure under your toe". If we played sinking down games, we would likely feel our shin against our boot. We don't need more than that – that is effective feedback.

Clear Intention – identified focus of **Attention** – followed by investigation of what you noticed. There is *no* better way of improving your performance. Any Olympian will confirm that.

Keep on experimenting it's fun.

7. Ski on platforms not edges - it's safer

You're on your way already!

This may surprise you; if you practise just these two or three things and get truly adept with them you will be a more technically proficient skier than over 90% of the skiers you see on the slopes. I know they all get down things but look *how*! Stiff straight legs; leaning back; looking like they've got their hands in their pockets; no proper platform; skis with no real grip; hardly even the vestige of an arc. Little control, even less grace, and not a little dangerous quite often.

It usually takes only two or three days for my pupils to get to feel comfortable with these first simple techniques on easy slopes. It takes longer to become skillful with them of course, and longer yet to do so on increasingly difficult slopes – but believe me *you're on your way already!* Skiers with built-in bad habits may take a little longer because they have to UN-learn first, and then learn.

Get good with my beetles and grapes on blue runs and you'll have red runs in your pocket. Get good on reds – and black runs will be within your capabilities. Be aware though it will take time to become *really* skilfull with them.

I'm entitled I think to promise you *certainty* of skill development no matter who you are – provided you put in the time and effort; skiing should be simple, but skilfull skiing takes most folk quite a while. It took me about six years and that was after I found a good teacher; prior to that I didn't make any progress at all. Be patient and you'll get your rewards. The process of slowly improving is where a great deal of the pleasure resides.

But what about my edges? I hear you cry.

You may recall that in the Introduction to this book I referred to the *tilted platform* that comes about when you push your ski and it meets with *snow resistance*. You may recall that I told you that everything that matters in skiing concerns the interface between the sole of the ski, and the snow. You then brace *against* the platform and get carried round the arc by the ski through the action of Mother Earth's resistance. (If you are interested the *force* she applies is centripetal force).

This is in total contrast to *edges!* Ski instructors, trainers, TV commentators and a host of others never mention *platforms*. All they ever talk about is 'edges'. I cannot think why – edges are not nice; they are the line defining where there used to be something and now there isn't. You can fall off them. They cut you. Who wants them?

You *cannot* ski on an edge despite all the excited shouting about "getting them on the edge"; "getting an *earlier* edge"; "being too *hard* on the edges" etc. I am unable to tell you what these seemingly macho phrases mean – probably nothing; they just sound "good". If anything they probably just mean that the ski needs to be tilted either more or less.

Forget about edges, use platforms they're much safer. If edges were what we need then the best things to have attached to our bindings would be a pair of machetes. They would not create a platform for you but look how long and sharp they are! What could go wrong?

There's more to it than Beetles and Grapes. Snow-moles give you better platforms!

Those skiers who have made the most of my coaching are the ones who were willing to spend all the time it took to really embed their "beetles and grapes" into their skiing.

But sooner or later we need to move on, if we want to get even better. And this is where I introduce you to a new little friend. So let's go child-like again. My next metaphor is the "Snow-Mole" and I'll shortly show how to put him to work.

The"snow-mole" helps improve the control you can exercise over the amount of *tilt* you get on your ski, and thus improves the reliability of the platform. As always, what we are seeking is ways to get a better platform so that we can obtain snow resistance for us to brace *against* as Mother Earth pushes our ski around the arc we want.

So, let's imagine again ....

"Snow-moles" are little furry creatures who love

skiers but are nervous because they don't yet know you and you may be one of the less skillful ones. They live under the snow until a skier comes along and then they pop-up and run along by the skier's side **in the second part of the arc** as you begin sinking onto your "grape". They only *ever* run along on the *outside* of the arc; never to the inside. This means once the arc begins to come across the slope your "mole" will always be on the *downhill* side. Very important, that.

Moles are cautious: they stay away to one side (the downhill side) of your outer ski, not staying too close in case of getting their ear chopped off. They also like to be tickled by really improving skiers so you now have a job to do.

With your outer hand (i.e. your left hand on a rightward arc, right hand on a leftward arc) you must reach *away to the side* and *down* slope (moles are small) to tickle your imaginary mole. You won't manage that if you reach out horizontally – it has to be *downslope.* You'll need to flex even more. Be careful to reach *away* from yourself, moles don't stay too close to your skis. My bet is that while this is very simple, at least at first you won't find it easy.

What then? As the arc is coming to an end your mole will run forward and duck under the snow to re-appear on the next arc to the outside of the next ski. Tickle him all the way until he disappears – which means that after you each *out* and *down* you follow-through *forward.*

What does this achieve?

Alright, we're playing childlike games, but they have grown-up rationale. They're childlike so that they'll come to mind easily next time we ski. But if you want reassurance that these games have real power, what does our "snow-mole" do for us?

If we successfully reach *out* and *down slope* to get to tickle his ears we will automatically move our hips – our centre of gravity – *up* the slope, and toward the centre of the arc our skis are describing. Your brain won't allow you to reach out and down so that you fall over. It simply won't allow it. Indeed its fighting against that is what makes this game initially hard to do.

An image of Usain Bolt comes to mind rounding the bend in a 200 mtr race. He isn't running upright, he's got his centre of gravity (somewhere roughly behind his navel) on the *inside* of the arc he's running. It's more difficult for *him* he hasn't got a snow-mole. Because he hasn't he tends to lean his entire body. We don't want to do that: as you get better at this you will be seeking to keep your torso vertical (looked at from the front), and your eyeline horizontal.

What happens is that because your hips move toward the arc's centre (and uphill in this instance) the ski that's supporting you will tilt slightly more. That will give you an even better *platform* to brace against. You will find that very beneficial and gives you a much safer feeling. My pupils always comment on how much "better" the arc feels. What they mean is more secure. More "grip", less slip.

So now you have three simple tools – a "beetle", a "grape", and a "snow-mole". Practise as much as you can, not only to learn how to do them, but *when* to do them.

Next – the Snow-mole’s friend ......

8. More strange snow creatures

"Snow Giraffes" – the snow-mole's best friend

Snow-moles get lonely when friendly skiers aren't around. Happily they have constant best friends – the "snow-giraffes".

Snow-moles get smaller and further away to the side as the slopes get steeper. (This is because the nutrients they need get washed away quicker so they get stunted, plus their fear that you may get too near and chop their ear off.)

Snow-giraffes on the other hand get taller as the slopes get steeper, because they don't have to bend down so far to get *their* grub which is uphill of them and this saves energy.

They too like to have their ears tickled. The snow-giraffes run alongside you on the **inside** of the arc. They accompany you for as long as the snow-mole does, and when you are *crossing* the slope they are uphill of you. There's no risk of your slipping upwards so the giraffes are less worried about having their ears cut off and are happy to be right next to you.

The key thing about snow giraffes is that not only have they longer legs than moles, they also have **longer necks. This is significant.** It means that as you tickle the ears of your snow-mole low down and away to the side of you, you'll tickle the ears of your snow-giraffe but **they will be farther forward than the snow-mole's.** There is of course a reason for this, to be revealed in a while.

It's all about adaptive posture.

I'm well aware that these images seem a bit silly: I also know that a good many ski school instructors would be unwilling to use them even if they knew about them. However in real skiing situations they **work.** These images are all concerned with helping you develop your Ready For Action posture *in an adaptive way* to suit the circumstances and to enhance your stability and security.

1. As you develop the ability to tickle the ears of your snow-mole and your snow-giraffe you will be positioning your hand carriage in the best way. Your outer hand will be low and out to the *side* of you – and always *slightly ahead* of you

2. and at the same tim you need to ensure your inner hand (tickling the giraffe's ears) will be somewhat *higher* than your outer hand (tall giraffe, short mole) and importantly *ahead* of your outer hand.

3. you'll move both of them forward when you're coming to the end of the arc just before each of them ducks under the snow to appear on the other

side during the next arc. This helps you avoid the risk of sitting back.

Look at any top rate skier and this will be noticeable. Even if you can't see their animal friends!

How long does the achievement of true expertise take?

Thus far I have introduced to you just three imaginary animals, and a 'grape'.

With nothing more than these, and with sufficient practice and possibly guidance from a coach, anybody unless in some way physically constrained by injury or ill-health, can become not just an 'advanced' skier, but an expert one. Anybody – including you: *especially* you because you have read this far and you are therefore one of the committed ones.

The steps in the progression that I have introduced to you so far would typically be covered in the first couple of weeks of any of my skiing courses. You would need rather longer to embed their use as habituated behaviours for you, but you would be well on your way.

Isaac Newton (1643 – 1727): his ski coaching years.

It seems so little – just three pretend animals and a store of grapes for them. Apparently child-like ideas.

Why do they work so well? The answer is "story telling" plus Isaac Newton and his physics.

I have mentioned before that we humans absorb information better if it is incorporated into narratives, and using analogies and metaphors. That's what my animals are all about.

Isaac Newton confirmed that any object in motion and having an established direction of travel will continue that motion and maintain that precise direction for ever – **unless acted upon by an externalforce.** There is nothing within the object's own system that can be done to change it; the force has to come from without.

Our external force is snow-resistance, which we obtain by having a ski which creates a **platform** that supports us, and against which we brace, because it is tilted. Not an "edge"!

Because you are standing in the centre of your ski and in motion, then as Mother Earth resists that motion, your ski will **bend** because the tips and the tails are more flexible than the middle. The force you are applying through the inertia of your mass operates in the centre of the ski because that is where you are attached.

Imagine you are skiing in a straight line with your skis flat on the snow: your mass is pushing downward and the snow is trying to push you upwards, by an equal amount. You are probably seated as you read this; your mass is acting downwards through your chair, and Mother Earth is resisting that with an *equal and opposite force*. You don't fall through the floor boards.

If your ski is *flat* on the snow (has no tilt) the snow-resistance will simply try to push it *upwards,* with a force exactly equal to the force you are exerting downwards. If on the other hand you *tilt* your ski, the snow resistance will act at an oblique angle instead of straight up, and will deflect the ski, pushing the tip to some extent laterally into what immediately becomes an **arc**.

If there were no friction at all as you ski, and no wind or any other resistance, neither your direction nor your speed would change. For ever. Newton said so. For the system to change you have to obtain some resistance from somewhere. Wind resistance would slow you down. Find snow resistance by pushing the snow, and it will push back. Do it with skill and it will push you where you want to go.

In the next chapter I will tell you how to best *use* your mole and your giraffe (and the door to their stables), to make changes of direction that will both look and more importantly *feel* like magic.

9. Skidding, the experts' way

SKIDDING – the recreational skier's best friend (and the back-country skier's as well).

The ski industry and an awful lot of instructors talk about little else but "carving". It is sold as "the way to ski", supposedly the ultimate aim of anyone with ambition. The manufacturers sell 'special' carving skis. It is the concern of much talk in the apres-ski bars. Yet again, I disagree. It can be great fun and very exciting but it's not the be-all and end-all and it gets to be very tiring. It's what the racers do and even they can't keep it up for long.

You can get your ski to do three things. You can get it to slide; or skid, or slip..

You can get it to **slip,** which is definitely NOT what you want. A 'slip' occurs when your ski doesn't go where it is pointing, and it has no tilt on it causing or allowing it to just slide away with you sideways pretty much uncontrollably. It can occur because a skier may "lean over" sideways having been (wrongly) told to "put your weight on the outside ski".

You can get it to **slide** – in a straight line known as a *schuss*, or along an arc (what the industry likes to call "carve"). In this instance the ski exactly follows in line with its arc – I'll explain shortly and it is more fully covered in my book "Ski In Control" available from Amazon. If you do all the things that precede this chapter in this book – you'll be "carving".

In a sliding arc, or *carve,* the ski will exhibit maximal *deflection* and minimal *deceleration.* Your ski will follow a perfect arc with no "scrubbing" action at all. This is precisely what racers want for example.

Now let's consider skidding.

You can get your ski to **skid.** A "slip" occurs through *reduction* of the tilt of the ski. A skid on the other hand is effected either by *not* reducing the tilt, or by increasing it *whilst simultaneously pivoting it across its direction of motion.* The ultimate *skid* would be the opposite of the ultimate "carve". It would slow you down the to maximum, and with *no* change of *direction* at all. You just keep going in the direction you were already going, and skid to a stop. You may have seen ice-hockey players come to a sudden stop by doing a "hockey stop" – that's an ultimate skid. Between those two lies an infinity of combinations of them.

I am going to examine skidding because not only is it one way to control your speed, (the other one being to wait as your ski carries you round an arc until it runs out of momentum) but skidding is also a way of skiing without too much physical effort and if you like to ski all day it will be of much benefit to you. Most folk do skid their skis, but few do it with precision; and many don't know they are doing it – it isn't deliberate. If you have an ambition to ski "in the bumps" then precision skidding is pretty much a pre-requisite unless you are a specialist bumps skier.

Pivoting your skis.

The example par excellence of pivoted-and-skidding skis, is "snow-ploughing" or "skiing in a wedge" when *both* skis are pivoted to some extent across your line of travel – ski tips close together, ski tails wider apart. At the same time, and because your feet will be wider apart than your hips, your skis will also be *tilted.* Because they are tilted they won't do the dreaded *slip!* We do snow-ploughing precisely to ensure that we ski slowly. Being skillful enough to be able to do it well is extremely valuable. And not very common.

You can use it on narrow tracks; in bad quality snow with crusty patches or hard-pack and you want to ski slower; and you can use it in a plethora of situations if you are off-piste or in the back-country. It is a technique with much to recommend it. It is also as Head of the Vail Ski School described it, "the best triangulated experimental platform you can get". Perfect for learning and *feeling* something new.

How to skid your skis.

Picture yourself skillfully using the techniques I've covered so far. Your skis are sliding cleanly round an arc – "carving". The tail of the ski is passing over exactly the same spot on the snow that the tip passed over. You have flexed at your ankle, your knee and your hip, and your dynamic posture is perfect but you are traveling faster than you would like.

You have two options – option 1, just WAIT until the ski carries you round enough of the arc for it to slow down by itself (with a well-executed arc it may well finish off by finishing *up*hill); – option 2 SKID it. But how? I want you to *imagine this* – feel yourself doing it. Two ways, best way first –

1. First way – (if say you are in a leftward arc) and mostly, perhaps entirely, supported by your right ski. Stand a *little* taller but still keep a forward sloping back. Then pivot your skis in a fairly fast movement a few degrees **to your left.** (Or to your *right,* if you're in a *rightward* arc.) The movement has to be fast only if you want to keep going in a straight line. This is not an easy thing to do – you will need to practice it. Keep your torso facing the way it **was.** Do it slowly and you will describe an arc. If you allow your chest or torso to continue facing your ski tips, you will also describe an arc – but at least probably a skiddy one.

2. Second way – make sure you are in a good Ready For Action posture, and the skis' tips are engaged with the snow, (don't be leaning back) and then push away in this case to the right (you're in a leftward arc) with both heels. This will pivot your skis around their tips, instead of the previous way when they would pivot somewhere around your bindings. This will set them parallel to one another but to some extent *across your line of*

travel . Again, for this to happen you must keep your torso facing the way it was – avoid letting it swing round with the pivoting skis. This is not an easy thing to do – you will need to practice it.

The inertia of your motion will now see to it that your ski continues to make an arc, but now your ski will be somewhat *across* your direction of travel and because it will still be tilted it will make a scraping sound, and it will offer more resistance to your motion and your speed will reduce. In this leftward arc example your skis will be pointing slightly more to your left than you will be traveling.

When might skidding be the best choice?

If you add a small amount of this 'pivoting' to all of your arcs, you will encounter less-strong forces from Mother Earth because your speeds will be lower and as a result you will need less muscular effort to *resist* those forces. Hence less-tiring skiing. An ability to selectively skid your skis is a huge benefit late in the day when all you want is to get back safely, and you wish you'd put in a bit less "carving" earlier!

The effect is for the ski to execute a wider 'drifting' kind of arc while you still maintain control. You will still be bracing *against* your outer ski because it will be tilted. What happens is that each arc loses you more height down the mountain, so you need fewer arcs to get home, and you use much less energy.

It's also a terrific technique when the light or the

conditions are poor – you ski slower and more safely, as well as having the benefit of being able to keep going longer.

PLUS – skidding is essential for skiing the “moguls” especially big ones sometimes encountered off piste in the back country. Some folk can “carve” them but not many and it’s a risky strategy when you’re along way from home. On narrow tracks skidding is very useful indeed – if you can’t do them in such circumstances in the ways described above – do them by snow-ploughing.

Get home safely!

10. "Carving" - fun but not all day!

Carving! Great fun – but tiring.

Being able to do do "carved" arcs on skis is very satisfying. It's also good fun. But it is also pretty hard work because your speed will be higher, the forces you have to resist will be greater, and for quite a time you may find your stress levels are higher because everything happens that bit quicker. Carving (or sliding) your ski is not for everyone.

As I've written earlier carving is just one technique. It's no more than that. It isn't *the* way to ski. This may be a good point at which to say that there isn't one way to ski – not for a skillful skier.

The whole thrust of what has gone before is that it prepares you for being able to ski in many and varied ways – as well as to "carve" – to suit you mood, and the conditions. The goal is – **all snows in all terrains**. We can leave the "one trick pony" act to somebody else. I can still remember the thrill I had the very first time I got to the bottom of a slope with the realisation that I could have selected from a number of different ways to have skied it. Prior that I had been a "one trick pony".

Carving is exciting and it's satisfying and it makes you look good, but I know of no-one who wants to do nothing else but. Too much like hard work!

The reason a ski "carves" or rather, *slides* is that a really good tilted platform has been created by you, and the ski is carrying you so cleanly around its arc that every point along its length goes over **the same snowflake** as the point just ahead of it.

This won't slow you down but it will give you an exceptionally stable and secure platform. Your velocity in this case is merely your choice; a high velocity does *not* mean a loss of safety. What makes you safer is knowing what you are doing and establishing a really good *platform* against which to brace.

Some key points about "carving".

The ski tip and its contact with the snow surface is, as ever, absolutely crucial. Think of your skis as being like restaurant waiters in a poorly paying restaurant – it's the tips that **really matter**! They initiate the platform by incising the snow surface and they generate the first deflection of direction .

Next comes our friend the 'grape'. To "carve" you must feel a lot of pressure directly on the grape – most of this comes from Mother Earth but she can't do it on her own. The result is that the entire length of the ski will distribute the load correctly, and the ski will bend (go into reverse camber) and this will define the arc's radius.

On many skis nowadays there is a cluster of numbers printed somewhere near the bindings. One of these tells you the exact radius that the ski's designer intended would be its optimum. It will do others, but this is when it is at its most precise. The ones I ski (and this is not a recommendation, they just happen to suit me) have a design radius of 19 metres for all-mountain use. Many specialise carving skis have radii of ten metres or less, but I can still get mine accurately carving when I wish to.

Because you will likely be traveling faster, you'll need to ensure a really first rate Ready For Action posture, and be ready for anything! Things come up on faster when you're carving. You will need to adopt a more flexed posture if you're carving fast – just look at racers to see what I mean.

11. What's next? It's up to you, the sky's the limit.

Where does all this get us? What's next?

This short book is designed to accompany and give added explanations to the series of YouTube videos on the Bobski Channel. I hope it has explained how – and most importantly why – my skiing coaching lessons are the way they are. It has been suggested (by others, not by me) that many ski instructors would serve their pupils better if they took on board some of these approaches.

No ski instructor, or coach can change your skiing – only you can do that. But what we can do is to ensure that you are given the right tools to do the job. Too often ski schools fail to do that. They tell you that you need to *watch* one of their often only partially qualified instructors skiing, and then copy what you think you saw. That simply doesn't work.

One of the reasons it doesn't work is that they don't help you to *understand* what happens when a ski slides over the snow. A disappointing number of the instructors produced by the organisations that provide them for ski schools don't *know* what happens. They can ski, some of them rather well and most of them better than I can, but you are not paying them to ski, you are paying them to help you learn.

Another reason is that far too often they teach the wrong things.

If they do know, then many of them fail to put it across to their pupils in readily comprehensible ways. Or perhaps inadvertently employ language that without their realising it, sets up their pupils in adverse psychological ways. I have in mind here the hard-to-notice effect that using words like "edges", and "fall-lines" have on many people.

We humans get good at what we *do* not what we *see*. As earlier chapters have I hope made clear, what we think we see when we watch a good skier is of little use. What actually works is what we *feel* and most importantly what we are *aware of* as *we* ski. This requires from your teacher that they watch you, not you watch them. My job is to watch you; your job is to *be aware*. Crucially therefore you need to be helped to appreciate of what it is do you need to *be* aware.

I have given you in this book a series of very simple *movements in motion* that you need to make in order to become the best you can be as a skier. I have couched them in seemingly child like ideas like 'snow-moles' and 'beetles' and I have clarified precisely why I have taken that route. I have also explained something it is highly unlikely any one else ever has – **how skis work**.

Over decades now I have proved, and coaches both more experienced and more advanced than I, have proved, that the "Intention/Attention Feedback loop" and enhanced awareness are without doubt the best way for you to become the kind of skier you want to be. The techniques of learning and of controlling your mind that I have deployed for you, are techniques used at the very highest levels of elite sports performance, not just in skiing but in every high level sport.

How long it will take you to become skillful at all of the preceding is anybody's guess. You may find that it takes almost no time at all. Others may take a holiday trip or three. Maybe more.

It really doesn't matter, and whatever it is it's no reflection on you. It isn't a race. What matters and what is really enjoyable is the *process*. It's like life really, if you don't appreciate the process you're missing rather a lot because finishing the "race" has an unfortunate outcome. Better to take your time.

However, here's the rub – when you *can* execute all of what is in these chapters, **you will be an accomplished skillful skier.** Maybe not expert yet but there won't be much you can't ski and fully control what happens. What is more, you'll ski twice as gracefully as over 95% of all the skiers you see on the slopes. You will have a skiing "toolkit" complete with techniques to enable you to ski in a wide variety of ways to suit your mood at the time. You will not be "a one-trick pony". And if that doesn't make you more proud of your self – I shall be amazed.

You don't have to ski fast. Speed isn't an issue unless you want it to be: grace and technical skill are not about speed, and neither is speed an indicator of skiing ability or control. The fact is, I could get a complete beginner to ski very fast indeed even on a gentle slope, it is all too easy. And would be dangerous.

But **only really competent skiers can ski very steep slopes slowly,** in complete control. To exercise that degree of control really takes skill. This is why you see so many skiers traveling fast on quite gentle slopes and scarcely making arcs at all – just taking almost a straight line down the piste: it's because they are poor skiers. They do not know what to *do*, almost certainly no one ever told them.

It's one of the reasons some of the tracks that join one piste to another can be so problematical. Poor skiers just ski straight down them with their hands in their pockets, standing straight upright, and going like bats out of hell. It's not an expression of expertise, it's because they can't do anything else.

Of course there is always more to learn, we can always get better. We can choose to be always on a pathway to being the best we can be. But if you have read this far, and if you have joined in with the practices I have explained, and if you have played these games sufficiently for *you* (and everybody is different in that respect) then you will ski black runs with confidence.

And as likely as not, that will be more than you expected.

THE FUTURE: What happens at higher speeds?

As you become more confident and your speeds increase things change somewhat. There comes a time when these excellent techniques you have been practising form the solid basis for a change in the *way* you will ski.

It opens up all sorts of good things and more odd ideas from me, such as “stable doors” leading to snow-mole and giraffe accommodation – “bouncing and floating” in the powder .... But that is for another day .... and probably another skiing course.

It’s part of the next stage in your development and I’m working on its provision. Stay tuned !

I hope you have enjoyed this trip as much as I have. Thanks for joining in. Good luck with your skiing.

The End.

This is where you can add appendices or other back matter.

Printed in Great Britain
by Amazon

78013044R00061